LIVING
OUT
OF YOUR
SPIRIT

DR. CARROLL PARISH

ISBN 978-0-9713462-6-0

CONTENTS

FOREWORD

The Bible says in 1 Thessalonians 5:23, 24, *"Now may the God of peace Himself sanctify you completely; and may your whole spirit, soul, and body be preserved blameless at the coming of our Lord Jesus Christ. He who calls you is faithful, who also will do it."*

Notice that this passage mentions three things that are part of the human makeup: spirit, soul, and body. We have the potential of living our lives under the influence of one or more of these three. Often, we vacillate from one to the other in the course of a week or even a day.

The Scriptures are clear that we should be living out of our regenerated spirit. By that we mean that the spirit should have the most influence over our actions, attitudes, words, etc. Too often we find that we live out of our mind, will, emotions, or the desires of the body.

In this little book we want to look at two areas. The first area deals with where God actually lives in our life; the second area is about how we can learn to live out of our spirit. These two areas of truth are life transforming. If we can master them we will become world changers never again to cower before the world, flesh, or devil. The voice of God will become dear to us. God working in and through us will become a regular occurrence. Loneliness will become a thing of the past. God's presence and power will become recognizable both in and upon our life.

Let's dive in and see what God can say to us!

CHAPTER ONE:
WHERE IS GOD?

Is He lost? Do we have to find Him? Has He been seeking us? Is God separate from His people? In the Old Testament we find God primarily as a God of majesty, power, and glory. Israel would get in trouble, repent, and call on God, and He would show up to spectacularly deliver them.

We wonder about a God like that. Where is He? In the midst of the times when we hurt or are in trouble, we often ask where is the God who did spectacular things for Isaiah, Jeremiah, or Daniel? Where is that God when I need Him?

Genesis 3:7, 8 tells us that God communed with Adam and Eve in the cool of the day; they experienced His nearness to them. But after the Fall they were excluded from the Garden of Eden. He no longer appeared near.

Is God still majestic and powerful? Yes, He is. His character **never** changes, but the way that He does some things **does** change based on the covenant you are living under.

Too many of us live on the wrong side of the Cross. That is, we believe that God is up there and we are down here and must handle things by ourselves.

If I were to question a Christian who believed that, no doubt he would soon agree with me. He might say, "Oh, no, I know that God is in me. But it sure seems like He is far off." Now we have two separate things. We have the way things *are* and the way things *appear* to be. Things may appear to be one way, but they may actually be a different way. I may feel that I am alone and that God has deserted me; but in fact, if I am a believer, He has not left me alone. He said, *"I will never leave you nor forsake you."* I may feel alone, but I am never alone on the terms of the New Testament.

If I am living under the terms of the Old Testament I only recognize the presence of God when He does something great, majestic, or spectacular because that is one of the major ways God dealt with people then. But things are different now because we are living under the terms of the New Testament. The book of Hebrews says that Jesus is the guarantee of the New Covenant (Heb. 7:22). The New Covenant is a better covenant established on better promises (Heb.8:6).

WHERE IS GOD TODAY?

So where is God today with the believers? 1 John 4:4 says, *"You are of God, little children, and have overcome them* [things in the world] *because He who is in you is greater than he who is in the world."* He is in you if you are a believer. He lives inside you. Wherever you go, you take Him with you—24/7. Wherever you are, whatever you are doing, whatever you are thinking, whatever emotions you have, whatever activity you are involved in, God is with you. If you feel His presence or power, God is with you. And if you are alone in the midst of a bad situation, He is still with you! He has not changed. He has not moved. He has not lessened His abilities, His desire, or His power. Greater is He who is **in** you than he that is in the world.

BECOMING GOD-INSIDE MINDED

We need to become so "God-inside minded" that it affects our attitudes, the way we think, and our actions every day. The world may be against you, but He is with you. If we understand that God is in us all the time, then we can realize that the Greater One does what needs to be done from within. We do not have to wait for Him to come down from heaven and meet our need. He is here within us.

Colossians 1:27 says, *"To them God willed to make known what are the riches of the glory of this mystery among the Gentiles: which is Christ in you, the hope of glory."* Notice this verse says that Christ is **in** you. He is in you **now**.

Look at Romans 8:9-11: *"But you are not in the flesh but in the Spirit, if indeed the Spirit of God dwells in you. Now if anyone does not have the Spirit of Christ, he is not His. And if Christ is in you, the body is dead because of sin, but the Spirit is life because of righteousness. But if the Spirit of Him who raised Jesus from the dead dwells in you, He who raised Christ from the dead will also give life to your mortal bodies through His Spirit who dwells in you."*

Verse 11 says, *"But if the Spirit of Him who raised Jesus from the dead dwells in you* [and, if you're a believer, He does], *if any man have not the Spirit of Christ, he's none of His."* So, if you belong to Jesus you have been regenerated in your spirit; His

Spirit has taken up residency inside you. *"He who raised Jesus from the dead will also give life to your mortal bodies through His Spirit who dwells in you."*

Historically, much of Christianity has interpreted that verse to mean "at the resurrection." If you die before Jesus returns and as part of the first resurrection, your body will be raised. It is the Holy Spirit that gets you out of the grave just like it got Jesus out. I believe that, but I do not believe that is all that it means. I believe the Spirit of God who lives in you 24/7 can quicken your mortal body, can give life to your mortal body TODAY. If your body needs it, the Spirit on the inside can release it into your mortal body.

God is out for our good all the time. He is trying to work in us and perfect us all the time. He is trying to conform us to the image of Jesus all the time. He wants us to be well and healthy all the time. This should change the way we think and live to realize that God is in us.

A NEW CREATION

1 John 3:2, *"Beloved, now we are children of God; and it has not yet been*

revealed what we shall be, but we know that when He is revealed, we shall be like Him, for we shall see Him as He is." As a child of God, you are a new creation. You are different than you used to be. You have Jesus living in you. Before you were born again, you had a dead spirit, but now you have a spirit that is alive with the life of God! Now you can both see and enter the Kingdom of God (John 3:3, 6) because you have King Jesus living in you! You have His Spirit in your regenerated spirit. From that position He can influence your life to the degree that you allow Him to do so.

A RENEWED MIND

To comprehend the greatness and majesty of having Jesus living in us is almost more than we can receive. It takes a mind renewed by the Word of God to be able to receive such truth. One reason for this is that we have often been taught how fallen mankind is. And without Jesus as Saviour we are fallen, depraved, spiritually dead, and blind. But having been born again in our spirit, we now have Him living in us. We are no longer old sinners, but now we are children of God. Now we are redeemed with the

Redeemer living in us. We have His life in us. We are alive in body, mind, and spirit.

We are told in Romans 12:2, *"And do not be conformed to this world, but be transformed by the renewing of your mind, that you may prove what is that good and acceptable and perfect will of God."* Notice that transformation follows renewal of the mind. The more "God-Inside Minded" we become, the more His presence and power will be seen outwardly! When individuals are not mindful of God living in them, they often feel that they have to do everything. They see their success or failure in life as being totally up to them. They are not able to live in the peace and rest that comes from living out of His Spirit instead of their flesh. The struggle to be spiritual, godly, or holy is constant because they, in their flesh, are fighting the battle without much reliance on the One who is in them.

But as one begins to see that by living out of his regenerated spirit a life heretofore unseen begins to be possible. Victory, joy, peace, and power begin to be manifested in all areas of his life. Fellowship with God is deepened and more intimate, and life is not just an existence, but an ongoing relationship with the risen Lord.

CHAPTER TWO:
THE POWER OF
IDENTIFICATION

In this chapter I want us to see how the things we identify with control our life. This is true whether it is good or bad, true or false. Our spiritual maturity, success, or failure in life, are all intertwined with whom or in what we find our identification.

THE POWER OF OUR PERCEPTION OF REALITY

Our perception of reality affects everything we believe. Do you believe God exists? Do you believe He is a good God? Do you believe that He is actively involved in your life? The answers we give to these questions will determine what our life will be like.

Reality is found in many dimensions, such as health, mental and emotional realms, financial and spiritual. Those who live their life according to what their natural eyes can see, or the other senses, will know only physical or external reality. But those who believe in God and a reality beyond the natural will know that what they see is only a portion of what total reality is. They can know that God is at work in the unseen realm to cause things to work out for their good even when the external circumstances do not look like they will. So the question is, whose reality will you believe?

We are told in 2 Corinthians 4:16-18, *"Therefore we do not lose heart. Even though our outward man is perishing, yet the inward man is being renewed day by day. For our light affliction, which is but for a moment, is working for us a far more exceeding and eternal weight of glory, while we do not look at the things which are seen, but at the things which are not seen. For the things which are seen are temporary, but the things which are not seen are eternal."* Notice the contrasts in these verses: outward—inward; seen—unseen; temporary—eternal. The outward, seen, and temporary are realities, but of a lesser quality than the inward, unseen, and eternal. Whichever reality we live by will determine the quality of life we have.

THE POWER OF AGREEMENTS

Because of our faulty perceptions we have often accepted as fact the experiences, ideas, and beliefs of others. By doing so, we are making an internal agreement with that thought or idea. Agreements we make bind us to that agreement and the power behind it. For example: if someone says to you or you think this about yourself, "You are no good—worthless," and you accept this thought as reality, it will cause your image of yourself to be limited to it. Perhaps a thought comes to you that says, "God doesn't love you," and you believe it; you will begin to see yourself as unloved and unlovable. If from past failures you think, "Others may be successful, but I will not," then you are to some degree setting yourself up for more failures. These types of perceptions about reality exist in every realm of our life. We need to examine our thought life and belief systems to determine where they are and begin to correct them.

There are four things that will be necessary to break wrong agreements and begin to establish a right view of reality. They are:

REPENT—acknowledge to God that you know you have some wrong views about Him, yourself, and the world around you. Ask for His forgiveness and accept it by faith.

RENOUNCE—the devil and his power that may be associated with the wrong agreements to the thoughts, ideas, and beliefs that you have accepted as reality. Tell him that you belong to God and that he has no right in your life.

REBUKE—him in Jesus' name. Tell him to go from you. Remind him that you are God's property, redeemed by the blood of Christ, and that he has to go from you.

REPLACE—the agreements and thoughts you have made with plain statements from the Word of God. Begin to read the New Testament, especially the epistles, where you are told who you are in Christ and what He has purchased and planned for you. Renew you mind in these truths, and you will experience freedom from Satan's dominion.

THE POWER OF IDENTIFYING WITH GOD AND HIS WORD

Philippians 4:8, 9 says, *"Finally, brethren, whatever things are true, whatever things are noble, whatever things are just, whatever things are pure, whatever things are lovely, whatever things are of good report, if there is any virtue, and if there is anything praiseworthy—meditate on these things. The things which you received and heard and saw in me, these do, and the God of peace will be with you."*

Notice three things that stand out from these verses:

PRINCIPLE— we need to meditate on right things.

PRACTICAL—we need to imitate someone who is doing it right. The best example is the Lord Himself.

PROMISE—God will be with you. While He is always with us because He lives in us, this seems to imply that His presence will be manifested among us in our circumstances.

How do our agreements with the world and wrong ideas of reality affect whether or not we live out of our spirit? The Bible answers that in Romans 8:5, *"For those who live according to the flesh set their mind on the things of the flesh, but those who live according to the Spirit, the things of the Spirit."* We can see from this verse that where and on what we think determines our walk with God. If we only see things from a natural or fleshly perspective, we will miss what God is doing and saying in our spirit.

His perspective on life will be left out of our life. We will be living, not out of our spirit, but out of our own thinking or the world around us. We will be living **in** the flesh.

Spiritual realities will be nonexistent for us as long as we live that way. Hearing the voice of God will be very difficult. There will be foggy thinking as it relates to divine revelation. Insight into spiritual things will be very shallow.

But that is not what God wants for us. He wants us to live out of our regenerated spirit so that we can hear the voice of God clearly. He wants us to know what His will for our life is. He wants us to walk with Him daily, fellowshipping with Him, and working with Him as He advances His Kingdom on the earth (2 Cor. 6:1). One of the ways we can do that is to cultivate hearing God in our spirit.

CHAPTER THREE:
HEARING THE VOICE OF GOD

I remember the first time I saw a transistor radio. A fellow student brought it to school, and when our teacher saw it she used it to explain radio waves. She explained that when a radio station broadcasts a program, the signals travel through the air and are picked up by a radio that is tuned to that frequency. If there are no radios tuned to that frequency, the signals are still in the atmosphere, but no one will hear them.

Psalm 19:1-4 says, *"The heavens declare the glory of God; and the firmament shows His handiwork. Day unto day utters speech, and night unto night reveals knowledge. There is no speech nor language where their voice is not heard. Their line has gone out through all the earth, and their works to the end of the world."*

A general revelation of God is seen in His creation. The Creator is seen through His creation. His creation speaks of His power, majesty, and glory. His voice is heard in it.

Psalm 29:3-9 says, *"The voice of the Lord is over the waters . . . the voice of the*

Lord is powerful, the voice of the Lord is full of majesty . . . the voice of the Lord breaks the cedars . . . the voice of the Lord divides the flames of fire . . . the voice of the Lord shakes the wilderness . . . the voice of the Lord makes the deer give birth."

Jesus, when speaking about Himself as the Good Shepherd, said in John 10:3, 4, 27 *"To him the doorkeeper opens, and the sheep hear his voice, and he calls his own sheep by name and leads them out. And when he brings out his own sheep, he goes before them; and the sheep follow him, for they know his voice. My sheep hear My voice, and I know them, and they follow Me."* Three times in this passage He says that His sheep hear His voice. The **"sheep hear his voice . . .** for **they know his voice . . . my sheep hear my voice."** Notice that He tells us that the end result of hearing His voice is following Him. If we are going to follow Him, then it is imperative that we learn to hear His voice. But how can we know how He will speak to us?

HOW GOD SPEAKS

There are at least ten ways God speaks to us. They are:

GOD SPEAKS THROUGH JESUS. This is the most important way of all. Heb.1:1, 2 says, *"God, who at various times and in various ways spoke in time past to the fathers by the prophets, has in these last days spoken to us by His Son, whom He has appointed heir of all things, through whom also He made the worlds."* The reason we say that this is the most important is because of who He is. He is the Son of God. He is Creator. He is Heir of all things. He is God revealed to man. He transcends everything! When He speaks we should learn to hear Him.

GOD SPEAKS THROUGH HIS WORD—THE BIBLE. In John 6:63 Jesus said, *"The words that I speak to you are spirit, and they are life."* The Word of God is of spiritual quality. It can be heard with physical ears, but understanding comes from the regenerated spirit because it is of the Holy Spirit.

Notice the power of the Word in Psalm 19:7-11, *"The law of the Lord is perfect, converting the soul. The testimony of the Lord is sure, making wise the simple. The statutes of the Lord are right, rejoicing the heart. The commandment of the Lord is pure, enlightening the eyes. The fear of the Lord is clean, enduring forever. The judgments of the Lord are true and righteous altogether. More to be desired are they than gold, yea, than much fine gold; sweeter also than honey and the honeycomb. Moreover by them your servant is warned and in keeping them there is great reward."*

Each of the terms used: *law, testimony, statutes, commandment, fear,* and *judgments* all refer to the word that emanates from the mouth of God. God is revealed by His Word. His will for us today is found in His Word. To hear the Word is to hear God speak. We need to cultivate a hearing ear that we might hear what He is saying to us from His Word.

Psalm 119:11, *"Your word I have hidden [treasured] in my heart, that I might not sin against You."*

Psalm 119:89, *"Forever, O LORD, Your word is settled in heaven."*

Psalm 119:105, *"Your word is a lamp to my feet and a light to my path."*

Psalm 119:130, *"The entrance of Your words gives light; it gives understanding to the simple."*

Psalm 119:165, *"Great peace have those who love Your law, and nothing causes them to stumble."*

GOD SPEAKS TO US THROUGH THE HOLY SPIRIT. Seven times in Revelation 2 and 3 God says to the churches in Asia, *"He who has an ear, let him hear what the Spirit says to the churches."* Just like there are radio signals in the air all the time, God is constantly speaking by His Spirit. Too often, we are tuned elsewhere and are not hearing what the Spirit is saying.

GOD SPEAKS THROUGH SPIRITUAL GIFTS. 1 Corinthians 14:1, 2 says, *"Pursue love and desire spiritual gifts, but especially that you may prophesy. For he who speaks in a tongue does not speak to men but to God, for no one understands him; however, in the spirit he speaks mysteries."* When one speaks in tongues, he speaks in the spirit. In fact, verse 14 says, *"If I pray in a tongue my spirit prays. . . ."* God can use the vocal gifts of prophecy, tongues, and interpretation of tongues to speak to us. He can use the other gifts such as the word of wisdom or the word of knowledge or any of the others, but the vocal gifts are the predominant ones. Praying in the spirit is a good way to cause one to become more spiritually alert to what is going on in his spirit. Often after a season of prayer he can hear

God speaking clearly. It isn't that He just started speaking, but through prayer one has tuned his spirit to His frequency.

GOD SPEAKS THROUGH MINISTRY GIFTS. Hebrews 1:1 says, *"God, who at various times and in various ways spoke in time past to the fathers by the prophets. . . ."* We have many examples in both Old and New Testament where God spoke to His people through prophets. He still uses this methodology. His nature has not changed, nor has His plan for His creation. Ephesians 4:11, 12 says, *"And He Himself gave some to be apostles, some prophets, some evangelists, and some pastors and teachers, for the equipping of the saints for the work of the ministry, for the edifying of the Body of Christ."* These are basically job descriptions for some in the church. God has chosen to use them to speak to and through them to His Body.

GOD SPEAKS THROUGH CIRCUMSTANCES. A good example of this is Jonah. God does use this method from time to time, primarily when we fail to hear Him speak through the other methods! It is less painful to hear God's voice through the Word and Spirit than circumstances.

GOD SPEAKS THROUGH AN AUDIBLE VOICE. Abraham and many others in the Bible can attest to this fact. Some in our day have given testimony of having heard God's audible voice. If He chooses to do so, He can still speak this way. However, it appears that this method was used primarily at times when the people did not have the Spirit living in them or were so spiritually dense that they could not hear God speak in their spirit.

GOD SPEAKS THROUGH DREAMS. Joseph is a good example of that. It was prophesied by the prophet Joel that in the last days God would pour out His Spirit and that old men would dream dreams. This sounds like it is still a viable method of hearing God.

GOD SPEAKS THROUGH VISIONS. The Apostle Peter is a good example of one who had a God-given dream. God spoke to him about going to Caesarea through a vision. In the prophecy given by Joel it also mentioned that young men would see visions.

COUNSEL OF A FRIEND. Proverbs 15:22 says, *"Without counsel, plans go awry. But in the multitude of counselors they are established."* Romans 15:14 says, *"Now I myself am confident concerning you, my brethren, that you also are full of goodness, filled with all knowledge, able also to admonish one another."*

The methodology that God uses to speak to us is important, but of less importance than the message He gives. We should be open and receptive to whatever method God uses to speak to us. Our heart's desire should be like one of old who said, *"Speak, for Your servant hears"* (1 Sam. 3:10).

RECOGNIZING THE VOICE OF GOD

The voice of God accomplishes very little in and through us if it is not heard. We need to learn to recognize God when He speaks to us.

We have to listen. Hebrews 11:6 says, *"But without faith it is impossible to please Him, for he who comes to God must believe that He is, and that He is a rewarder of those who diligently seek Him."* We have to believe that God does indeed speak today. We need to expect Him to speak to us. We have to listen for Him to speak.

To listen implies that some things we hear have to be disregarded, while other things become more important. In a crowded room with friends there are a lot of conversations going on. It is impossible to hear and keep up with all of them. We develop the ability to disregard some and to tune in to the ones we want to hear. This needs to be carried into the realm of hearing God.

In the 1970's I was pastoring a rural church in Western Kentucky. I had been there about two years. We had some successes, but also a lot of problems in the church. I was extremely frustrated and wanted to move somewhere else. I asked God to move me. I got no response from Him about it. A friend of mine pastored in St. Louis. His church was growing, and he invited me to come there and become his associate pastor. I really wanted to do it. I prayed about it, and I heard the Lord say that He wanted me to stay where I was. I prayed again, hoping that the Lord would change His mind. He responded each time I brought it up to Him with the same answer. The way He made me know what He wanted me to do was through the Scripture in John 10:11, 12 which says, *"I am the good shepherd. The good shepherd gives his life for the sheep. But a hireling, he who is not the shep-*

herd, one who does not own the sheep, sees the wolf coming and leaves the sheep and flees; and the wolf catches the sheep and scatters them." He asked me, "Are you a shepherd or a hireling?" I answered, "Lord, I am a shepherd." He responded then, "Stay with these sheep until I tell you to go."

About two years later while still pastoring that church I felt in my spirit that my time there was drawing to a close. One night I had a dream, and in the dream I saw two men sitting on our couch saying that they wanted me to come to their church and be their pastor. In the dream they told me the size of the church, and it was double the size of the one I was pastoring. They told me the salary, and it was 66% more than I was presently making. About two weeks after having the dream I got a phone call from a man in Tennessee who said that he and a friend would like to come talk to me about their church. When they came, everything was exactly like I had dreamed. After prayer, my wife and I felt that God was directing us to move to that church and assume the pastorate.

We will have to get on His frequency. We need to go to the areas where He is speaking. For example, God is heard more clearly through the Word in church than He is in the local bar. God is heard from His Spirit in more power in prayer than He is through a sporting event. God is heard through His ministry gifts rather than a medium or witch. We need to tune our hearts to His voice.

We need to learn to listen to Him in our spirit. Revelation 1:10 says, *"I was in the spirit on the Lord's Day and heard behind me a loud voice, as of a trumpet."* John was in tune with his spirit, and he heard God speak to him. He was in an attitude of listening. His spirit was open to God. He was yielded to God, and he heard Him speak.

To enable us to hear more clearly, here are some things we can do.

1. Ask questions. What are You saying to me, Lord? What do You want me to do? When do You want me to do it? How should I do what You want? God never gets angry with us when we ask for clarification about directions from Him.

2. Be quiet and listen. It is hard to hear His voice when we are always talking.

3. Check out what you hear with Scripture. Is it consistent with the Word of God?

If it is contrary to the Word, it did not come from God.

4. If you are still unsure if this is genuinely the voice of God, ask a more mature Christian for his opinion or prayer.

5. Be willing to adjust your course of action. Isaiah 1:19 says, *"If you are willing and obedient, you shall eat the good of the land."* If we hear something from God, we must be willing to adjust our plans accordingly.

KNOW THE DIFFERENCE

1 John 4:1 says, *"Beloved, do not believe every spirit, but test the spirits, whether they are of God; because many false prophets have gone out into the world."* While we are thinking about hearing the voice of God, it is important to realize that every voice you hear is not from God. All of us hear voices of some type. Some are thoughts, ideas, and voices from the world in which we live. Others come from the dreams or goals we are pursuing. Some of the voices, hopefully most of them, come from God. But there are some voices that are picked up that are not from God, but from the devil. These are the ones that we

need to be on guard against. The writer of 1 John indicates that one way to know if this voice comes from God or the devil is to determine if that voice, or belief system, acknowledges that Jesus has come in the flesh. In other words, what does it believe about Jesus? Who is He?

This becomes increasing important when we realize that in the last days there will be an increase in demonic activity even to the point of satanic miracles (Rev. 16:13, 14). I think it would be good to read the entire book of 1 John and other places in the Bible that speak to this issue.

CHAPTER FOUR:
LIVING OUT OF YOUR SPIRIT

In attempting to live out of our regenerated spirit, we are daily tempted to revert back to the way we used to live before regeneration. There seems to be something in all of us that has a tendency to do that. It is called the flesh. It is that part of our being that is not yet submitted to the Lordship of Christ. The Apostle Paul deals with it in depth in Romans 7. He tells us about the struggle to do the things we know we should be doing, and yet at the same time something tries to keep us from doing it.

Paul says in Romans 8:9, 10, *"But you are not in the flesh but in the Spirit, if indeed the Spirit of God dwells in you. Now if anyone does not have the Spirit of Christ, he is not His. And if Christ is in you, the body is dead because of sin, but the Spirit is life because of righteousness."* Even though this struggle between flesh and Spirit exists, believers are "classified" as NOT being in the flesh but in the Spirit because the Spirit of God lives in them. This is seen also in

Paul's letter to the Galatians. In spite of the trouble that existed in the churches in that region between some who wanted to go back in Judaism, Paul still referred to some of them as spiritual. Galatians 6:1 says, *"Brethren, if a man is overtaken in any trespass, you who are spiritual restore such a one in a spirit of gentleness, considering yourself lest you also be tempted."* We learn from this that being spiritual, or living out of the spirit, is not the absence of conflict, but making the right choices.

WORKS OF THE FLESH OR FRUIT OF THE SPIRIT

Galatians 5:19-21 lists the works of the flesh. They are: *"adultery, fornication, uncleanness, lewdness, idolatry, sorcery, hatred, contentions, jealousies, outbursts of wrath, selfish ambitions, dissensions, heresies, envy, murders, drunkenness, revelries, and the like; of which I tell you beforehand, just as I also told you in time past, that those who practice such things will not inherit the Kingdom of God."* These are the normal things that occur in one's life who does not live out of his regenerated spirit. Notice that this letter was written to the churches in

Galatia. It is specifically addressed to believers. It is possible for us to commit such sins if we do not follow the directions of the Spirit of God.

Now notice what Paul said about the fruit of the Spirit in Galatians 5:22, 23, *"But the fruit of the Spirit is love, joy, peace, longsuffering, kindness, goodness, faithfulness, gentleness, self-control, against such there is no law."* These verses tell us what is produced in and through us when we yield to the Spirit of God.

LED BY THE SPIRIT

Romans 8:14 says, *"For as many as are led by the Spirit of God, these are sons of God."* It is expected behavior for believers to be led by the Spirit of God. It should not be thought unusual to see someone being directed by the Spirit of God. This should be commonplace for believers. To hear God speaking to us, to have daily communication with Him, to recognize His promptings, although supernatural, should be regular occurrences in our life.

Galatians 5:18 says, *"But if you are led by the Spirit, you are not under the law."* Many people in the region of Galatia were going back to Judaism from Christianity. Paul is trying to show them that real freedom is found in being led by the Holy Spirit. 2 Corinthians 3:17 says, *"Now the Lord is the Spirit, and where the Spirit of the Lord is, there is liberty."* Only those who are led by the Spirit know the freedom and liberty of the Kingdom of God.

These leadings or promptings of the Spirit are not relegated to Sunday or church meetings. They should be happening daily in business, home, school, and recreational settings. They should occur in health, financial, and all other areas of our life. God wants to lead us. We have been created with a place for Him to live in us. Our human spirit was made with this in mind. Our entire human makeup is suited for God to live in, and through our life to accomplish the work of His Kingdom.

WALKING IN THE SPIRIT

Paul says in Galatians 5:16, *"Walk in the Spirit and you shall not fulfill the lusts of the flesh."* The word "walk" in Greek is *peripateo,* which means "to conduct oneself, to regulate one's life." To walk in the Spirit then would consist of conducting your life under the direction of and obedience to the Holy Spirit. Notice that he says as we are doing this we will not be fulfilling the lust of the flesh. The fruit of the Spirit will be manifested instead.

To walk in the Spirit means that He has the freedom to invade our life and direct us where He chooses. Since we are His property (1 Cor. 6:19, 20) He has the legal right to do so. But He will not intrude where He is not welcome. If we make a choice to go contrary to His leadings, He will allow us to do so. He will speak to us through the Word. His Spirit will send people to us to speak a word of encouragement about following God. He will use various means to get us to do His will. But if we choose the flesh instead of the Spirit, He will allow it. But the end results of the flesh will become evident at some point. We will not experience the benefits of the Kingdom of God. On the other hand, if we follow the direction of His Spirit in us, we will have the love, joy, and peace that come with walking with God. The Kingdom of God (Romans 14:17) will be flowing in and through us. The most successful place to be is in the will of God, walking with God through the Spirit from within.

Galatians 5:25 says, *"If we live in the Spirit, let us also walk in the Spirit."* If we are spiritually alive in our spirit—we are if we are born again—let us walk in the Spirit. It is saying that as surely as we are new creations in Christ, we need to walk in the Spirit. Some people put a lot of emphasis on the New Birth, but very little emphasis on walking with God thereafter. But this verse is showing us how important it is to continue to establish ongoing fellowship with God.

THE PLACE OF SPIRITUAL GIFTS

The Apostle Paul, in setting the gifts of the Spirit in order in the Corinthian church, had this to say in 1 Corinthians 12:7, *"But the manifestation of the Spirit is given to each one for the profit of all."* God gives spiritual gifts to His Body. These gifts are manifested through individuals in the church. The purpose of the gift is not to lift up that person, but to build up the Body and meet human needs.

Paul, after giving a listing of some of the spiritual gifts, also said in 1 Corinthians 12:11, *"But one and the same Spirit works all these things, distributing to each one individually as He wills."* It is the will of

God for each person in the church to have one or more spiritual gifts through which God works for the profit of all. Notice this verse says He distributes His gifts to each one individually. That says to me that you have a gift of God on the inside of you. It resides in your spirit where the Spirit of God resides.

The gift of the Spirit, regardless of type, flows out of the Spirit from within. Notice some passages where Paul seems to indicate this. 1 Corinthians 14:2, Paul in the context of teaching on speaking in tongues says, *". . . In the spirit he speaks mysteries."* 1 Corinthians 14:14 says, *"For if I pray in a tongue my spirit prays. . . ."* 1 Corinthians 14:15 says, *"What is the conclusion then? I will pray with the spirit, and I will also pray with the understanding. I will sing with the spirit, and I will also sing with the understanding."*

Jude 20 says, *"But you beloved, building yourselves up on your most holy faith, praying in the Holy Spirit."* As we pray in the Spirit our human spirit is expressing the mind of God. We are praying about things that our natural mind cannot fathom. We are soaring above where our human understanding stops. The Spirit of God is finding expression and often interceding about things that we have not yet known. We are truly living out of our spirit when we pray in the Spirit!

THINGS THAT WILL HELP US LIVE OUT OF OUR SPIRIT

Some of the same things we mentioned that will help us hear the voice of God better will also help us live out of our spirit.

As we renew our mind with the Word of God, we are being transformed (Rom. 12:2). God works in agreement with His Word. As we read, meditate, memorize, and acknowledge the Word, we are being transformed. We are gradually moving from selfish ambition and exaltation to humility through His work in our soul. We are constantly being more tuned in to His voice and will for our life. We become more spiritually aware of what He wants to do.

As we abide in God and His Word abides in us, we have great freedom in prayer (John 15:7). Prayer does not draw God closer to us, but it makes us aware of His presence. I am sure that all of us at one time or the other has experienced the manifest presence of God after an intimate time of prayer. The prayer did not make God leave heaven and come down to us; it merely made us more sensitive in spirit to His presence within us.

If you have a prayer language (speak in tongues), use it much. I have discovered over the years that as I pray in my prayer language, it opens the door into the supernatural in a greater way.

Obedience to what God says to us will also make us more sensitive to future words from Him. When they ran out of wine at the wedding feast in Cana in Galilee, Jesus' mother told the servants, *"Whatever He says to you, do it"* (John 2:5). This is still good advice today!

OTHER BOOKS BY
DR. CARROLL PARISH

BECOMING WHO YOU ARE—$3.00

This book shows who we are in Christ and who He wants to be in us. There are 168 things that He has provided for us through the Cross. They are all referenced in this little book.

**TURNING THE CURSE INTO
BLESSING**—$3.00

Curses operate in everyone's life to some degree. In this book we discover how we can turn the curse around and be blessed instead.

**THE MOST OFTEN GIVEN
COMMAND**—$3.00

Of all the commands in the Scripture, there is one that is given more often than the others. This book is about how you and I can obey this command every day in every circumstance.

SICK AND TIRED—$3.00

This book is about what you can do to regain your health by using natural means, or stay healthy by diet and lifestyle.

CONTACT INFORMATION:

Dr. Carroll Parish
3402 Goose Creek Road
Louisville, Kentucky 40241
(502) 426-3132